Ready·Set·Learn . . . .

Consonants

150+ Stickers Inside

Blends

cub	club flag
plant	fish
paint	globe
back	black
play pay	

Managing Editor
Ina Massler Levin, M.A.

Editor
Eric Migliaccio

Contributing Editor
Sarah Smith

Creative Director
Karen J. Goldfluss, M.S. Ed.

Cover Design
Tony Carrillo / Marilyn Goldberg

Teacher Created Resources, Inc.
6421 Industry Way
Westminster, CA 92683
www.teachercreated.com
ISBN 13: 978-1-4206-5934-4
©2007 *Teacher Created Resources, Inc.*
Made in U.S.A.

Teacher Created Resources

This book belongs to

_____

Ready·Set·Learn

2

Get Ready to Learn!

Get ready, get set, and go! Boost your child's learning with this exciting series of books. Geared to help children practice and master many needed skills, the *Ready·Set·Learn* books are bursting with 64 pages of learning fun. Use these books for . . .

 enrichment   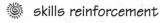 skills reinforcement   extra practice

With their smaller size, the *Ready·Set·Learn* books fit easily in children's hands, backpacks, and book bags. All your child needs to get started are pencils, crayons, and colored pencils.

A full sheet of colorful stickers is included. Use these stickers for . . .

☀ decorating pages

☀ rewarding outstanding effort

☀ keeping track of completed pages

Celebrate your child's progress by using these stickers on the reward chart located on the inside cover. The blue-ribbon sticker fits perfectly on the certificate on page 64.

With *Ready·Set·Learn* and a little encouragement, your child will be on the fast track to learning fun!

Bb

Directions: Color the pictures that begin with the *b* sound.

1.	2.	3.
4.	5.	6.
7.	8.	9.

4

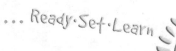

More Bb

Directions: Say the name of the picture. Circle the beginning sound.

1.	**2.**	**3.**
b c	d b	b f
4.	**5.**	**6.**
g b	b h	d b
7.	**8.**	**9.**
b c	d b	f b

Cc

Directions: Say the name of the picture. Listen for the beginning sound. Write the letter.

1.	2.	3.
4.	5.	6.
7.	8.	9.

More Cc

Directions: Draw a line to connect the pictures that have the same beginning sound.

Dd

Directions: Color the pictures that begin with the *d* sound.

1.	2.	3.
4.	5.	6.
7.	8.	9.

More Dd

Directions: Say the name of the picture. Circle the beginning sound.

1.	2.	3.
d c	d c	d f
4.	5.	6.
g d	d h	d b
7.	8.	9.
d c	d b	f d

Ready·Set·Learn

Ff

Directions: Say the name of the picture. Listen for the beginning sound. Write the letter.

1.	2.	3.
4.	5.	6.
7.	8.	9.

More Ff

Directions: Draw a line between the pictures with the same beginning sound.

Gg

Directions: Color the pictures that begin with the *g* sound.

1.	2.	3.
4.	5.	6.
7.	8.	9.

12 ©Teacher Created Resources, Inc.

More Gg

Directions: Say the name of the picture. Circle the beginning sound.

1.	**2.**	**3.**
g c	b g	f g
4.	**5.**	**6.**
g d	g b	h g
7.	**8.**	**9.**
c g	d g	g f

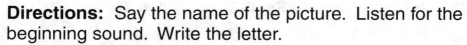

Hh

Directions: Say the name of the picture. Listen for the beginning sound. Write the letter.

1.	2.	3.
4.	5.	6.
7.	8.	9.

More Hh

Directions: Draw a line to connect the pictures that have the same beginning sound.

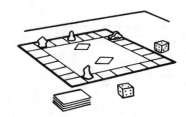

Jj

Directions: Color the pictures that begin with the *j* sound.

1.	2.	3.
4.	5.	6.
7.	8.	9.

More Jj

Directions: Say each picture. Circle the beginning sound.

1.	2.	3.
j c	j g	f j

4.	5.	6.
d j	j b	h j

7.	8.	9.
g j	j d	f j

Kk

Directions: Say the name of the picture. Listen for the beginning sound. Write the letter.

1.	2.	3.
4.	5.	6.
7.	8.	9.

More Kk

Directions: Draw a line between the pictures with the same beginning sound.

Ll

Directions: Color the pictures that begin with the *l* sound.

More Ll

Directions: Say the name of the picture. Circle the beginning sound.

1. l   j
2. g   l
3. f   l
4. l   d
5. b   l
6. h   l
7. k   l
8. c   l
9. l   k

Mm

Directions: Say the name of the picture. Listen for the beginning sound. Write the letter.

1.	2.	3.
4.	5.	6.
7.	8.	9.

More Mm

Directions: Draw a line to connect the pictures that have the same beginning sound.

Nn

Directions: Color the pictures that begin with the *n* sound.

1.	2.	3.
4.	5.	6.
7.	8.	9.

More Nn

Directions: Say the name of the picture. Circle the beginning sound.

1. n m	**2.** g n	**3.** n f
4. d n	**5.** n b	**6.** NOODLES h n
7. k n	**8.** n c	**9.** m n

Pp

Directions: Say the name of the picture. Listen for the beginning sound. Write the letter.

1.	2. PAINT	3.
4. PASTE	5.	6.
7.	8.	9.

More Pp

Directions: Draw a line to connect the pictures that have the same beginning sound.

Qq

Directions: Say the name of the picture. Listen for the beginning sound. Color the pictures that begin with the *q* sound.

1.

2.

3.

4.

5.

6.

7.

8.

9.

Rr

Directions: Color the pictures that begin with the *r* sound.

1.	2.	3.

4.	5.	6.

7.	8.	9.

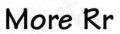

More Rr

Directions: Say the name of the picture. Circle the beginning sound.

1. r m	2. n r	3. r f
4. d r	5. r b	6. h r
7. r k	8. c r	9. m r

Ss

Directions: Say the name of the picture. Listen for the beginning sound. Write the letter.

1.	2.	3.
4.	5.	6.
7.	8.	9.

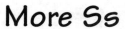

More Ss

Directions: Draw a line to connect the pictures that have the same beginning sound.

Tt

Directions: Color the pictures that begin with the *t* sound.

1.	2.	3.
4.	5.	6.
7.	8.	9.

More Tt

Directions: Say the name of the picture. Circle the beginning sound.

1. b t	2. t c	3. d t
4. t f	5. g t	6. h t
7. t j	8. k t	9. l t

Vv

Directions: Say the name of the picture. Listen for the beginning sound. Write the letter.

1.	2.	3.

4.	5.	6.

7.	8.	9.

More Vv

Directions: Draw a line to connect the pictures that have the same sound.

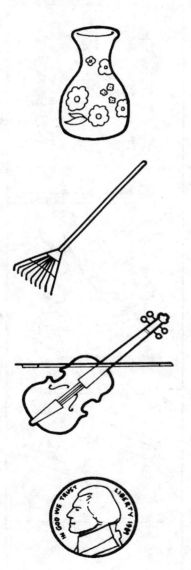

36

More Ww

Directions: Color the pictures that begin with the *w* sound.

1.	2.	3.
4.	5.	6.
7.	8.	9.

More Ww

Directions: Say the name of the picture. Circle the beginning sound.

1.	**2.**	**3.**
w v	t w	w s
4.	**5.**	**6.**
r w	q w	w p
7.	**8.**	**9.**
w n	m w	w l

38   ©*Teacher Created Resources, Inc.*

Xx, Yy, and Zz

Directions: Color the pictures that begin with the *x* sound red. Color the pictures that begin with the *y* sound yellow. Color the pictures that begin with the *z* sound blue.

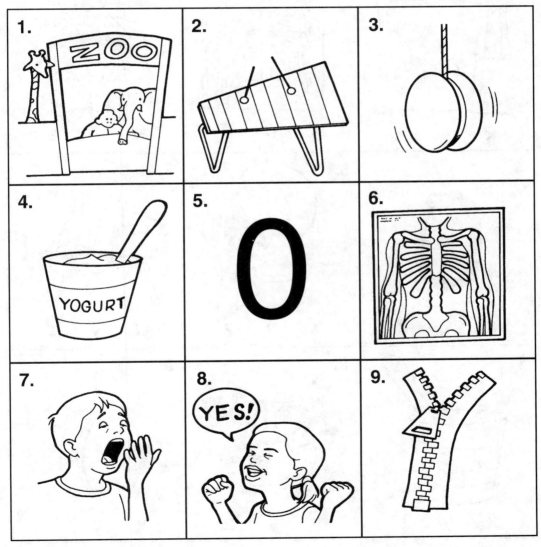

1.
2.
3.
4.
5.
6.
7.
8.
9.

More Xx, Yy, and Zz

Directions: Say the name of the picture. Circle the beginning sound.

1. ZOO x y z	**2.** x y z	**3.** x y z
4. O x y z	**5.** x y z	**6.** x y z
7. YOGURT x y z	**8.** x y z	**9.** x y z

40

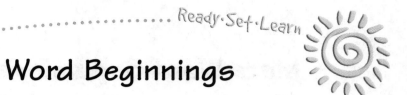

Word Beginnings

Directions: Say the sound of each letter. Think of a word that begins with each letter. Write the word on the line.

b

c

d

f

g

h

j

k

l

m

More Word Beginnings

Directions: Say the sound of each letter. Think of a word that begins with each letter. Write the word on the line.

n

p

q

r

s

t

v

w

x

y

z

Consonant Beginnings

Directions: Write the correct consonant on the line to spell the word the picture shows.

1.	2.	3.
____ an	____ ap	____ ub
4.	5.	6.
____ en	____ og	____ in
7.	8.	9.
____ un	____ eb	____ ot

Consonant Endings

Directions: Write the correct consonant on the line to spell the word the picture shows.

1.	**2.**	**3.**
ba ____	cu ____	nu ____
4.	**5.**	**6.**
do ____	lo ____	pi ____
7.	**8.**	**9.**
tu ____	mo ____	we ____

Missing Consonants

Directions: Write the correct consonants on the lines to spell the word the picture shows.

1. ___ i ___	2. ___ o ___	3. ___ e ___
4. ___ e ___	5. ___ u ___	6. ___ o ___
7. ___ a ___	8. ___ e ___	9. ___ u ___

R Blends

Directions: Say the name of each picture. Circle its name.

1.	2.	3.
brush rush	tuck truck	grape grin
4.	**5.**	**6.**
track truck	prince pin	fruit suit
7.	**8.**	**9.**
crib crab	grin grapes	train track

More R Blends

Directions: Name each picture. Write the letters for the beginning blend on the line. Then trace the whole word.

_____
- - - - - - oceries

_____
- - - - - - esent

_____
- - - - - - iangle

_____
- - - - - - idge

_____
- - - - - - incess

_____
- - - - - - agon

S Blends

Directions: Say the name of each picture. Circle the correct word that spells its name.

1. ski sing	**2.** net nest	**3.** sled send
4. slide slow	**5.** stamp stomp	**6.** spoke smoke
7. sway swing	**8.** star stone	**9.** stamp stump

More S Blends

Directions: Say the name of each picture in the first column. Circle each picture in the row that begins with the same blend as the first picture.

L Blends

Directions: Say the name of each picture. Circle its name.

1. plug plum	2. glove love	3. flame flop
4. mouse blouse	5. clip clam	6. clown crown
7. flat flute	8. globe robe	9. plant plate
10. class clap	11. blocks locks	12. flag flower

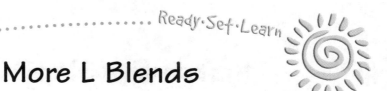

More L Blends

Directions: Read each word. If it begins with a blend, color the petal.

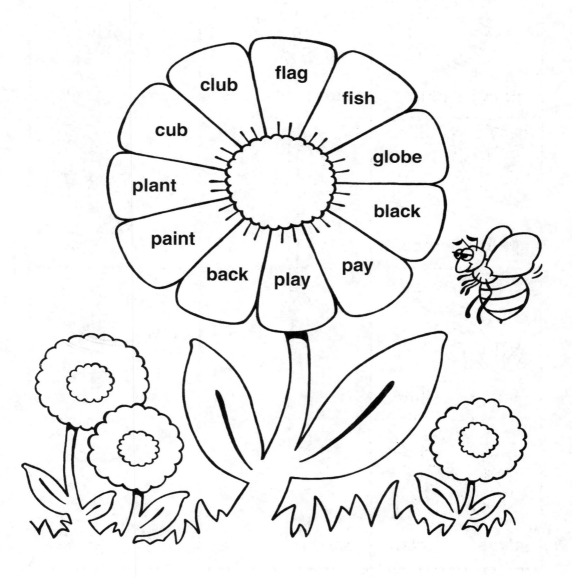

Match the Blends

Directions: Say the name of each picture. Draw a line to the letters that represent its blend sound.

sl

gl

gr

fl

cl

bl

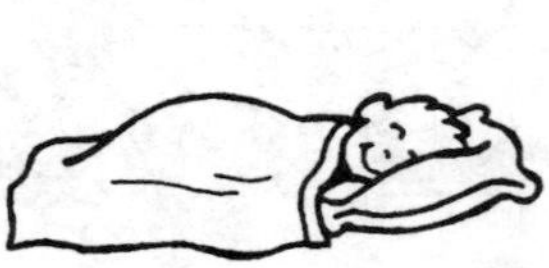

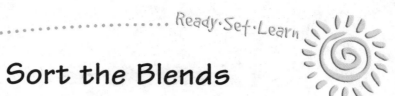

Sort the Blends

Directions: Read each word. Divide the words by blend. Write each word in the correct column. Circle the blend.

dragon	globe	star	swim	spider	stop
swing	frame	present	crown	truck	block
plant	bridge	clap	smoke	glue	crib
stone	clam	sponge	play	grape	flame

r blends	l blends	s blends

Final Blends

Directions: Say the name of each picture. Circle its name.

1.	2.	3.
west nest	bank tank	list fist
4.	**5.**	**6.**
most coast	junk bunk	mink rink
7.	**8.**	**9.**
rink think	wink sink	west vest

More Final Blends

Directions: Blend the letter sounds as you say each word. Then color the picture it names.

1. w ⟶ ing	
2. s ⟶ ing	
3. r ⟶ ing	
4. k ⟶ ing	
5. sw ⟶ ing	

Ch Words

Directions: Name each picture. Print the missing letters to complete the word.

1. imp	**2.** erries	**3.** eeks
4. ain	**5.** eese	**6.** in
7. air	**8.** ocolate	**9.** eck

Sh Words

Directions: Say the name of each picture. Circle its name.

1. shark / short / wash	**2.** shark / short / wash
3. sharp / shower / shingle	**4.** show / shop / shower
5. shut / shuttle / shed	**6.** fish / ship / flash
7. shop / shot / ship	**8.** shout / shade / shim

Th Words

Directions: Say the name of each picture. Color the sections that have pictures with the beginning sound of *th*.

58

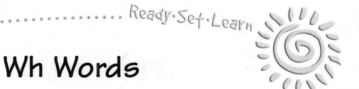

Wh Words

Directions: *Wheel* begins with the sound of *wh*. Color the wheel section if the picture in it begins with the sound of *wh*.

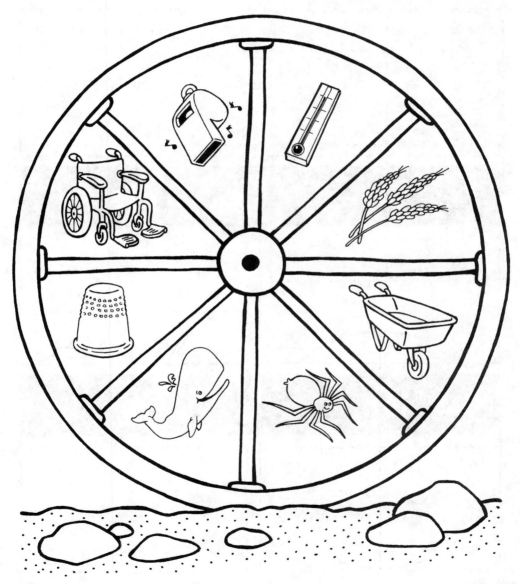

©*Teacher Created Resources, Inc.*   59   *#5934 Consonants*

Word Sorting

Directions: Read each word below. Print each word in the correct box.

path	chick	shout	what	thing
thread	math	push	gush	chin
chart	short	tooth	shelf	whale

sh

ch

wh

th

Identifying Digraphs

Directions: Read the word in the first column. Write the digraph in the second column. Fill in the bubble in the third column to show if the digraph is heard at the beginning, in the middle, or at the end of the word.

Digraphs			
ch	sh	th	wh

Word	Digraph	Position in Word		
		Beginning	Middle	End
1. chalk	ch	●	○	○
2. match		○	○	○
3. father		○	○	○
4. mouth		○	○	○
5. wash		○	○	○
6. lunch		○	○	○
7. sheep		○	○	○
8. teacher		○	○	○
9. whale		○	○	○

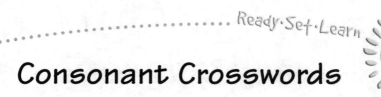

Consonant Crosswords

Directions: Name each picture. Write its name in the crossword puzzle next to it. Use the words in the box.

plus	flag	bride	frog
fly	fries	plug	broom

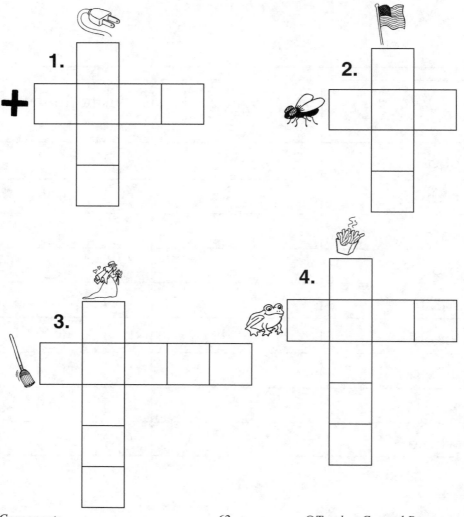

This Award
Is Presented To

_____

for

★ Doing Your Best

★ Trying Hard

★ Not Giving Up

★ Making a
Great Effort